Cambridge Young Learners English Tests

Cambridge Movers 1

Examination papers from

University of Cambridge
ESOL Examinations:

English for Speakers of Other Languages

CAMBRIDGE UNIVERSITY PRESS
Cambridge, New York, Melbourne, Madrid, Cape Town, Singapore,
São Paulo, Delhi, Dubai, Tokyo, Mexico City

Cambridge University Press
The Edinburgh Building, Cambridge CB2 8RU, UK

www.cambridge.org
Information on this title: www.cambridge.org/9780521693400

© Cambridge University Press 2007

This publication is in copyright. Subject to statutory exception
and to the provisions of relevant collective licensing agreements,
no reproduction of any part may take place without the written
permission of Cambridge University Press.

First published 1999
Updated edition 2007
3rd printing 2011

Printed in Italy by L.E.G.O. S.p.A.

A catalogue record for this publication is available from the British Library

ISBN 978-0-521-69340-0 Student's Book
ISBN 978-0-521-69341-7 Answer Booklet
ISBN 978-0-521-69342-4 Cassette
ISBN 978-0-521-69343-1 Audio CD

Cambridge University Press has no responsibility for the persistence or
accuracy of URLs for external or third-party internet websites referred to in
this publication, and does not guarantee that any content on such websites is,
or will remain, accurate or appropriate. Information regarding prices, travel
timetables and other factual information given in this work is correct at
the time of first printing but Cambridge University Press does not guarantee
the accuracy of such information thereafter.

Cover design by David Lawton
Produced by HL Studios

Contents

Test 1
    Listening   4
    Reading and Writing   10

Test 2
    Listening   24
    Reading and Writing   30

Test 3
    Listening   44
    Reading and Writing   50

Speaking Tests
    Test 1   65
    Test 2   69
    Test 3   73

Test 1
Listening

Part 1
– 5 questions –

Listen and draw lines. There is one example.

Fred   Daisy   John   Sally

Paul   Jill   Jane

Listening

Part 2
– 5 questions –

Listen and write. There is one example.

	Name:	Jill Walker
1	Lives at:	7 .... Street
2	Class number:	....
3	Favourite sport:	....
4	Likes reading:	....
5	Pet:	....

Part 3
– 5 questions –

What did Jane do last week?

Listen and draw a line from the day to the correct picture.

There is one example.

Monday

Tuesday

Wednesday

Thursday

Friday

Saturday

Sunday

Part 4
– 5 questions –

Listen and tick (✓) the box. There is one example.

What is Jill wearing?

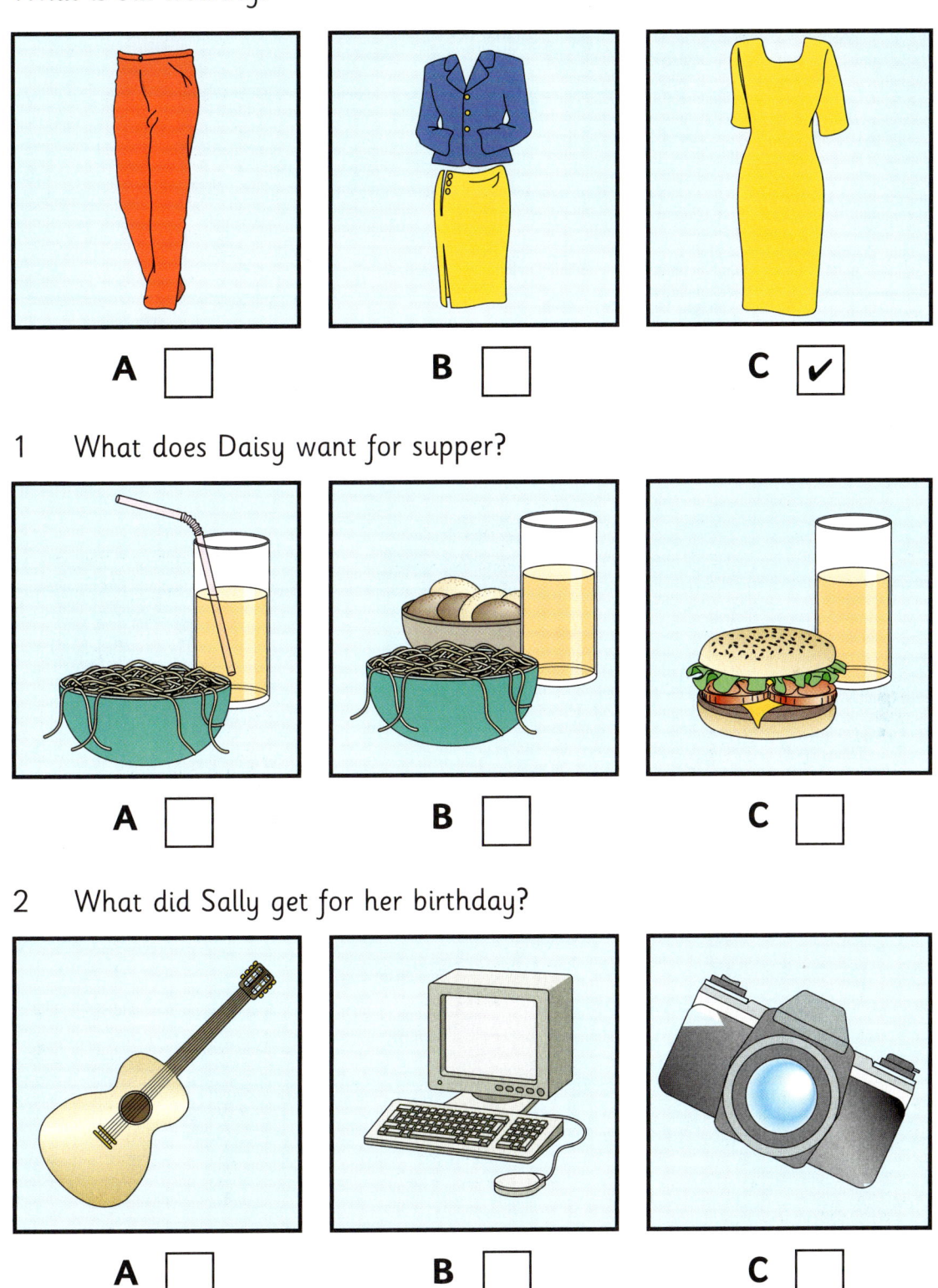

1 What does Daisy want for supper?

2 What did Sally get for her birthday?

Test 1

3   Where did Peter go at the weekend?

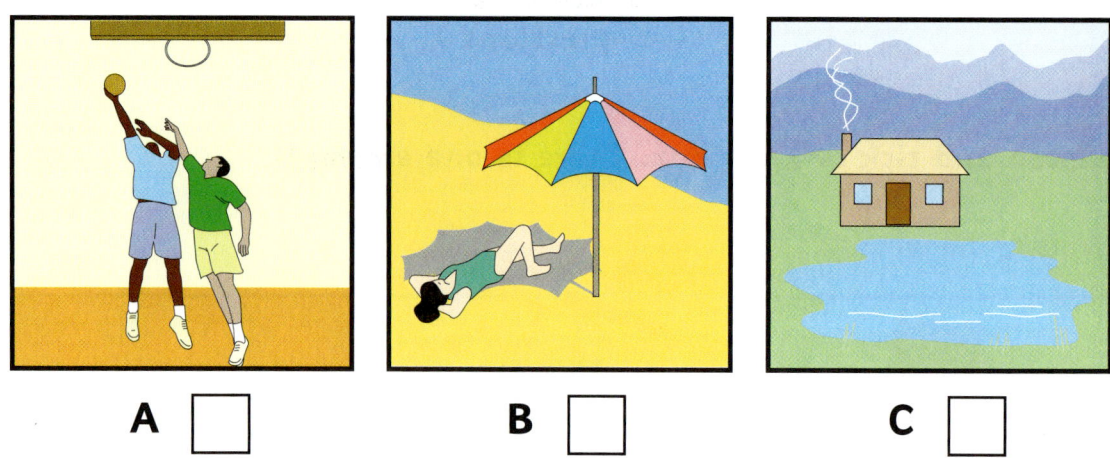

A ☐   B ☐   C ☐

4   What was the matter with Mary?

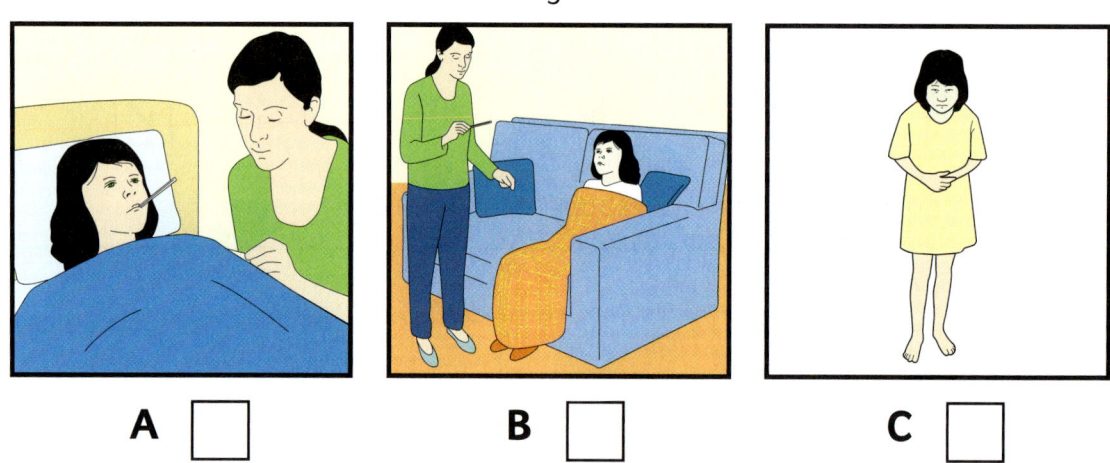

A ☐   B ☐   C ☐

5   What fruit has Fred got in his garden?

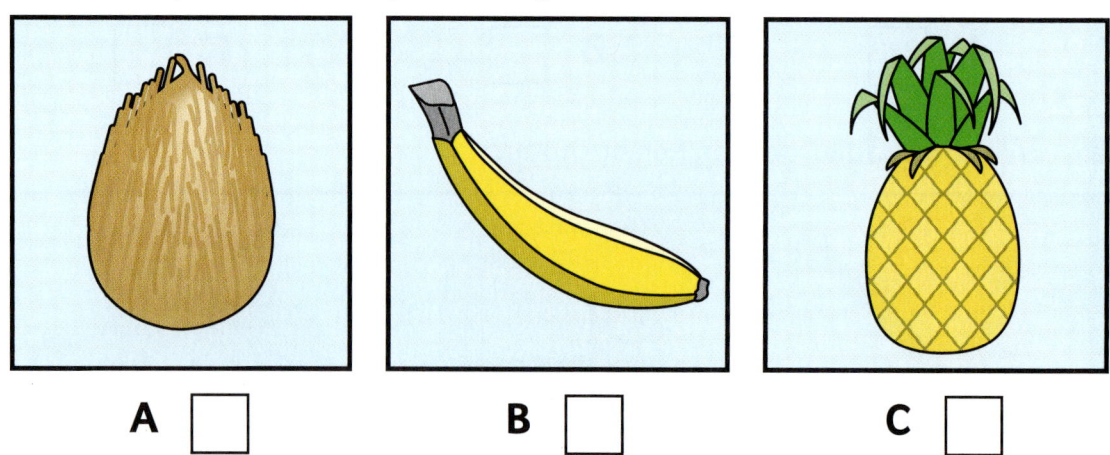

A ☐   B ☐   C ☐

Listening

Part 5
– 5 questions –

Listen and colour and draw. There is one example.

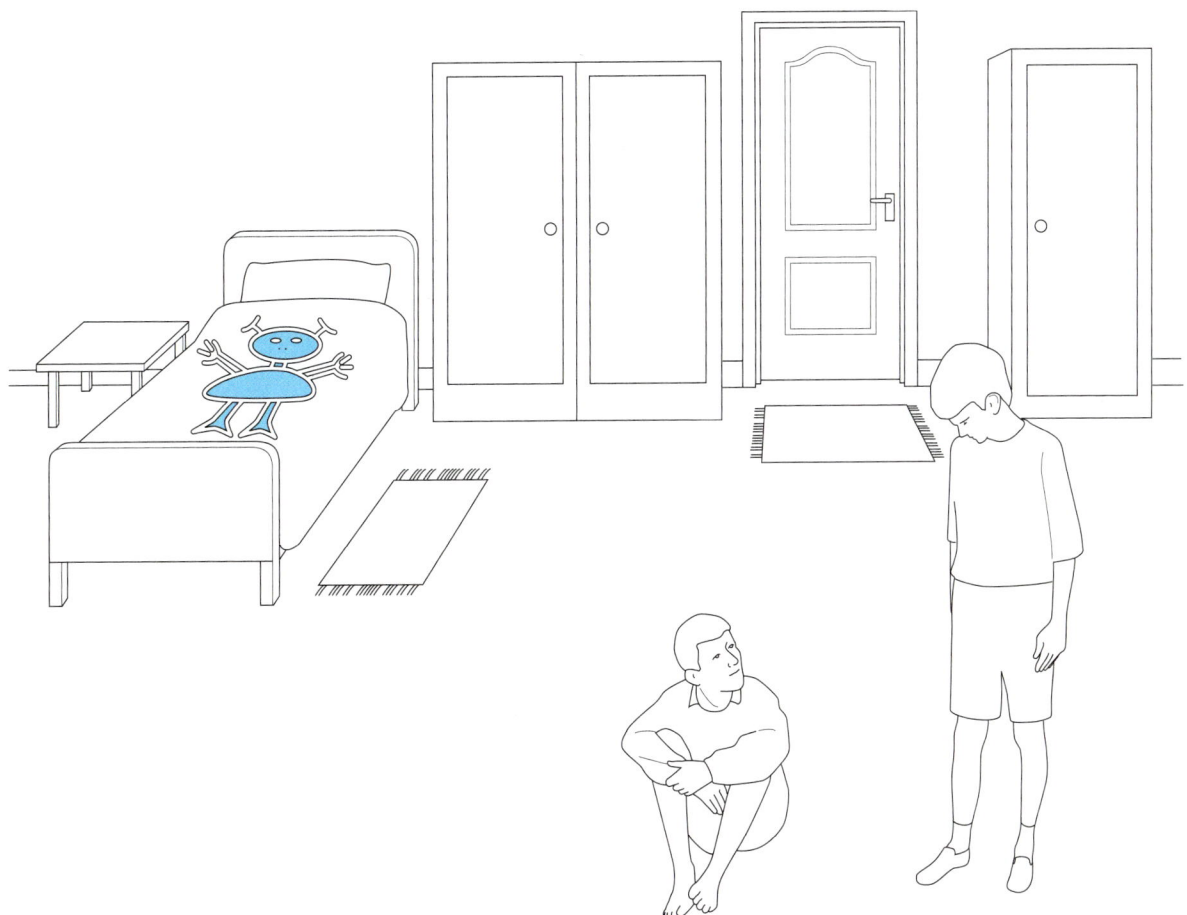

Test 1
Reading and Writing

Part 1
– 6 questions –

Look and read. Choose the correct words and write them on the lines. There is one example.

a library

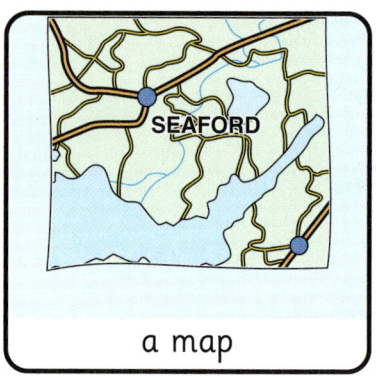
a map

blankets

a bookcase

a playground

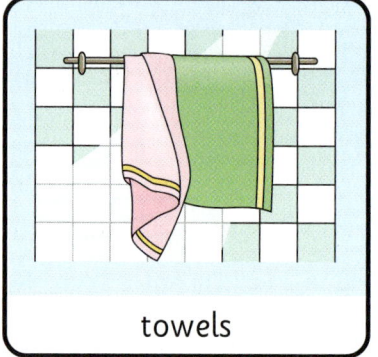
towels

homework

a park

Reading and Writing

Example

You put your books in this at home. ....*bookcase*.............

Questions

1   This helps you find the right road.   ....

2   You can play here between lessons.   ....

3   You go to this place to choose books.   ....

4   You put these on your bed on cold nights.   ....

5   You need one of these after a bath.   ....

6   You do this after school for your teacher.   ....

Test 1

Part 2
– 6 questions –

Look and read. Write yes or no.

Examples

The monkey which is in the tree
is eating some fruit. ....yes..................

The red and yellow bird is sitting
on a tree. ....no..................

Reading and Writing

Questions

1 The tiger is looking at a monkey. ....

2 The fat snake is climbing a tree. ....

3 Two crocodiles are swimming in the river. ....

4 One of the elephants is drinking in the river. ....

5 Three bats are flying under the trees. ....

6 The tall man has got a beard and a big hat. ....

Part 3
– 6 questions –

Read the text and choose the best answer.

Example

Jill: How are you today, Peter?

Peter: A It's very good.
(B) Fine thanks, Jill.
C I'm ten.

Questions

1 **Jill:** I didn't see you last weekend.

Peter: A No, we went to my aunt's house.
B Yes, I'm going home.
C No, we go to the supermarket.

Reading and Writing

2 **Jill:** Did your sister go with you?

  Peter: A No, she hasn't got one.
            B No, he went with us.
            C No, she couldn't go.

3 **Jill:** Has your aunt got any children?

  Peter: A Yes, she is.
            B Yes, she's got three.
            C Yes, she was.

4 **Jill:** Where does she live?

  Peter: A In the country.
            B In the river.
            C In the mountain.

5 **Jill:** Can I come with you next weekend?

  Peter: A No, I can't come.
            B Oh, OK then.
            C Yes, you do.

6 **Jill:** Oh, I must go home now.

  Peter: A Good evening.
            B OK, bye.
            C Well, hello.

Part 4
– 7 questions –

Read the story. Choose a word from the box. Write the correct word next to numbers 1–6. There is one example.

Last Saturday afternoon, I went to the cinema with my father. On the ....wall............ outside the cinema, there was a big picture of the film. We went inside. Dad **(1)** .... our tickets and an ice cream for me, then we sat down. The film was about a famous **(2)** .... His name was Jim and he had a curly, brown moustache! He **(3)** .... on a boat to an island with some friends. They ate some coconuts which they found on the **(4)** .... there, then they went fishing. After that, Jim went for a walk and found a big box between some rocks. He opened it and inside there was a lot of **(5)** .... ! Jim shouted to his friends, 'Come and **(6)** .... at this!' They all laughed and danced when they saw inside the box. I enjoyed the film a lot.

Reading and Writing

Example

(7) Now choose the best name for the story.
Tick one box.

A day at the shops ☐

An afternoon with Dad ☐

A morning lesson ☐

Part 5
– 10 questions –

Look at the pictures and read the story. Write words to complete the sentences about the story. You can use 1, 2 or 3 words.

Jane doesn't like shopping!

At the weekend, Jane's mum said, 'I want to go shopping. Can you help me Jane?' 'Yes,' she said. Jane and her mother caught a bus to the town. Jane's mother carried one bag and Jane carried another. The bus stopped outside a big supermarket and they went inside. Jane wasn't very happy. She thinks shopping is boring.

Examples

Jane and her mother went shopping ......*at the weekend*......... .

They went to town by ......*bus*......... .

Questions

1   Jane carried a .... for her mother.

2   They went shopping in the big ....

3   Jane doesn't enjoy shopping
    because she thinks it's ....

Reading and Writing

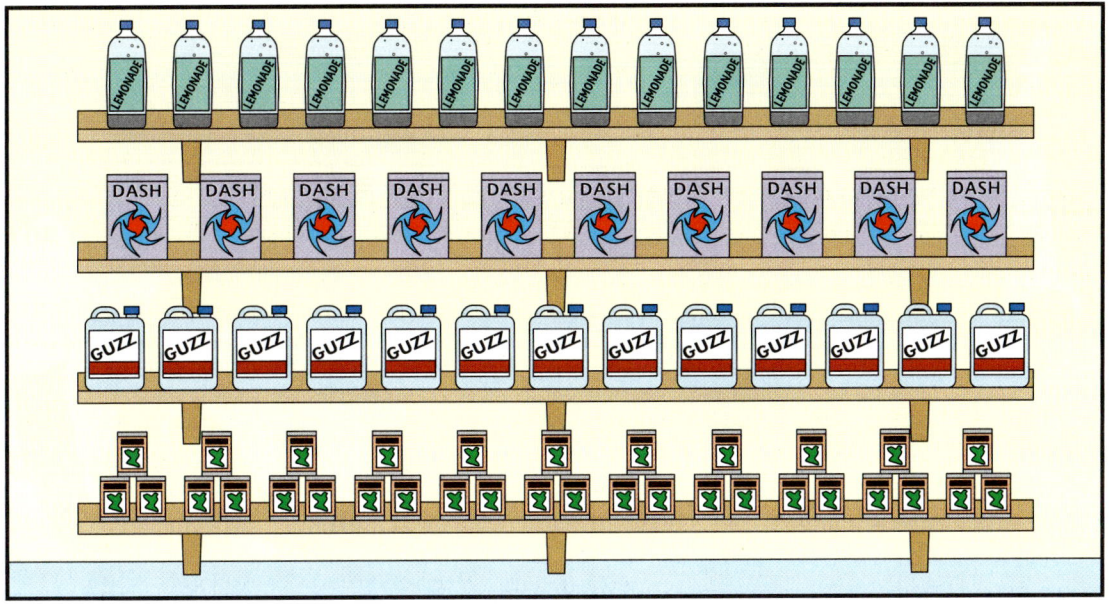

Inside the shop, Jane's mother picked up fruit and bread but she couldn't find any rice. But Jane found some below the pasta. Her mum was pleased. 'Clever girl!' she said. Then Jane's mother wanted a bottle of lemonade. Jane went to look. The bottles were in a difficult place but Jane climbed on a big box and took one. When she jumped down again, she hurt her leg and started to cry.

4   ………………………… found the fruit and bread in the shop.

5   The rice was under ………………………… .

6   Jane climbed on a box to get a ………………………… .

7   Jane started ………………………… because she hurt her leg when she jumped down.

Test 1

Jane's mother bought Jane a pink ice cream. She sat down and ate it. She stopped crying but her leg hurt and she could only walk very slowly on it. Jane's mother phoned home and Jane's father came to the supermarket to drive them home. When they got back, Jane's mother said, 'Oh dear! I can't take you shopping again.'
Jane smiled when she said that!

8   Jane's mother gave Jane a ....

9   Jane could not .... quickly because her leg hurt.

10 .... took them home again in the car.

Blank Page

Part 6
– 5 questions –

Read the text. Choose the right words and write them on the lines.

Dolphins

Example	Dolphins live in the sea. ......**They**...... can swim very quickly
1	.... catch a lot of fish. They are much smaller
2	.... whales or sharks, but more beautiful.
3	Dolphins .... come to the beach in hot weather
4	and play .... the children who are swimming there.
	They are not afraid of people.
5	You can often see dolphins .... zoos now.
	They learn how to play games with balls and toys. Dolphins are a lot of people's favourite animal.

Reading and Writing

Example	It	They	The
1	and	but	because
2	that	than	then
3	before	after	sometimes
4	with	of	at
5	by	in	to

Test 2

Listening

Part 1
– 5 questions –

Listen and draw lines. There is one example.

Mary   Ben   Tom   Paul

Jane   Anna   Pat

Part 2
– 5 questions –

Listen and write. There is one example.

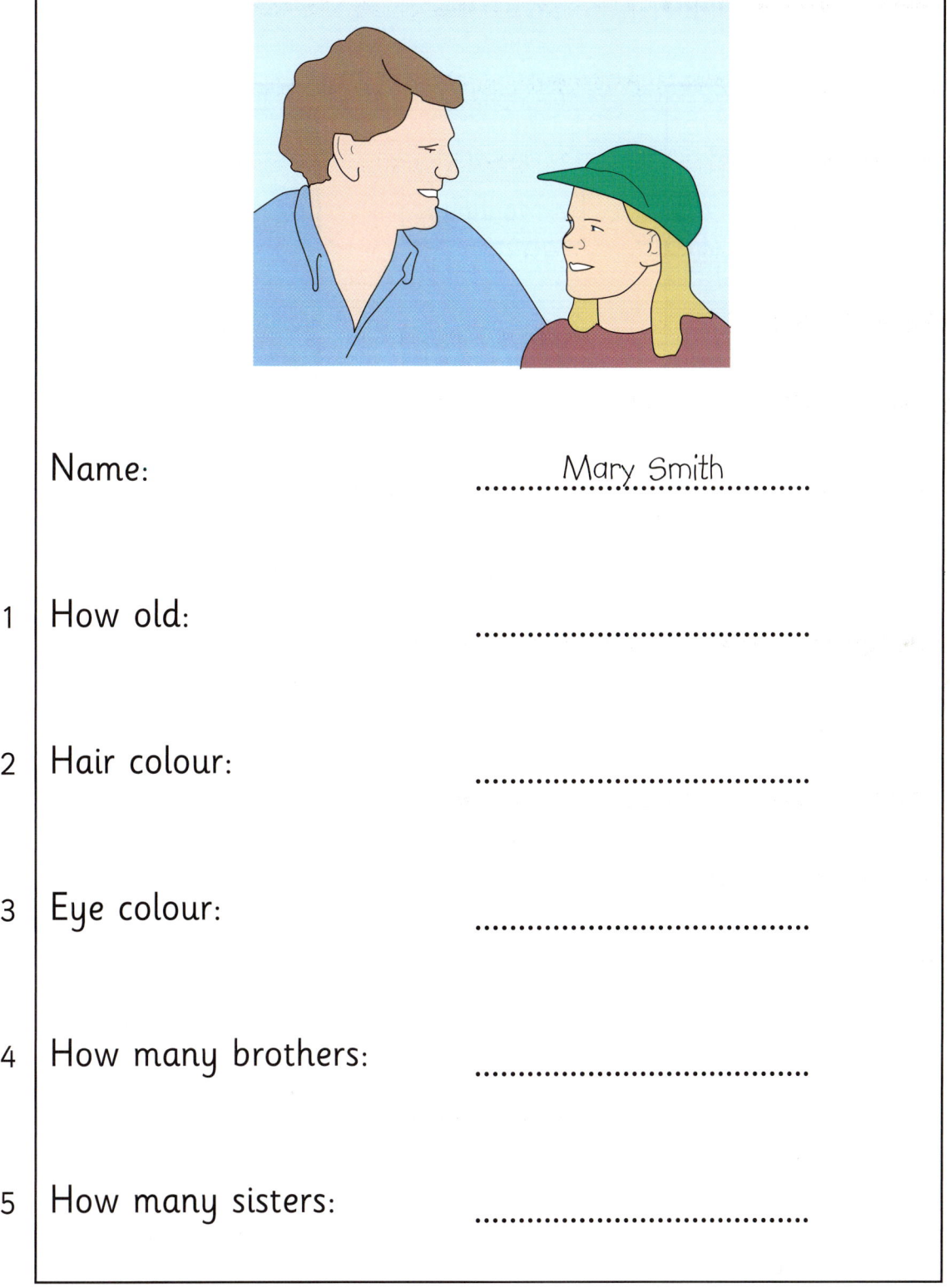

Name: ....Mary Smith............

1 How old: ....

2 Hair colour: ....

3 Eye colour: ....

4 How many brothers: ....

5 How many sisters: ....

Part 3
– 5 questions –

What did Paul do last week?
Listen and draw a line from the day to the correct picture.
There is one example.

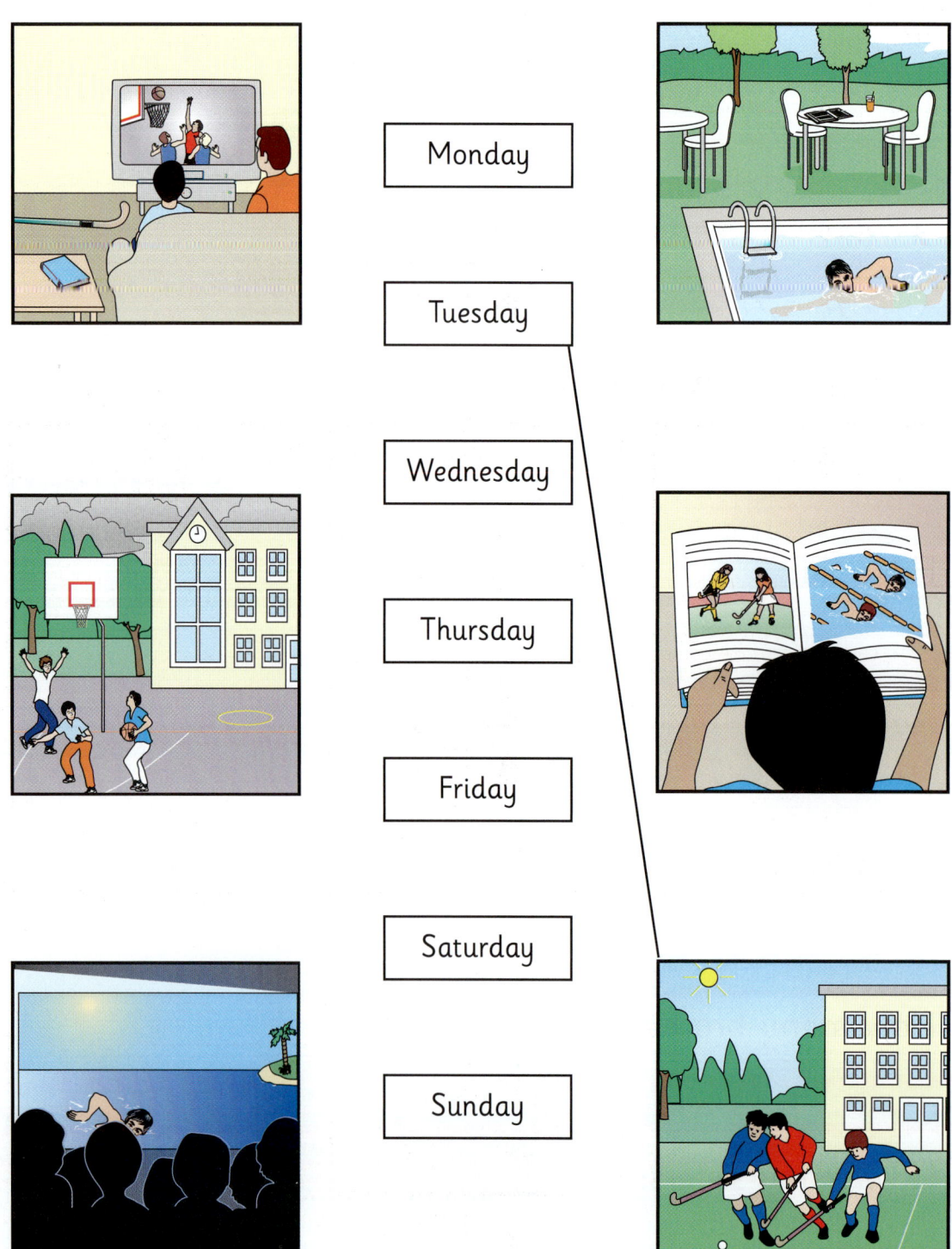

Listening

Part 4
— 5 questions —

Listen and tick (✓) the box. There is one example.

Where is Pat's dad going?

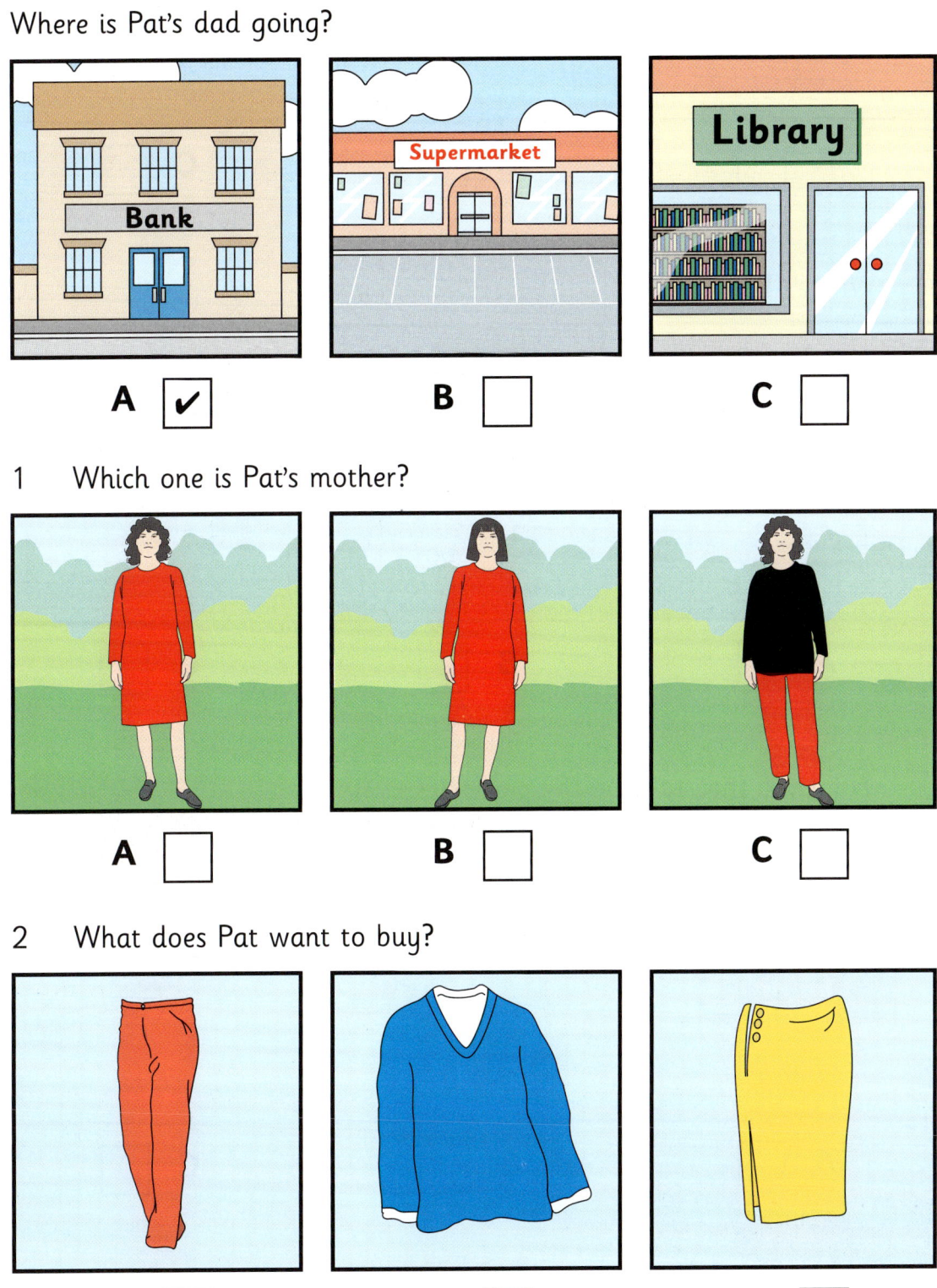

1 Which one is Pat's mother?

2 What does Pat want to buy?

3 What was the weather like here yesterday?

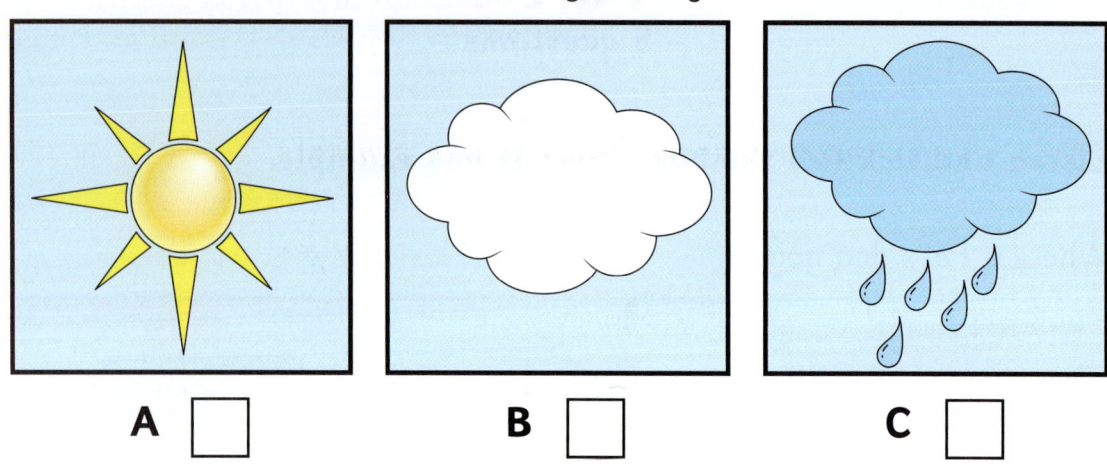

A ☐   B ☐   C ☐

4 Where's Peter?

A ☐   B ☐   C ☐

5 What will they take on the picnic?

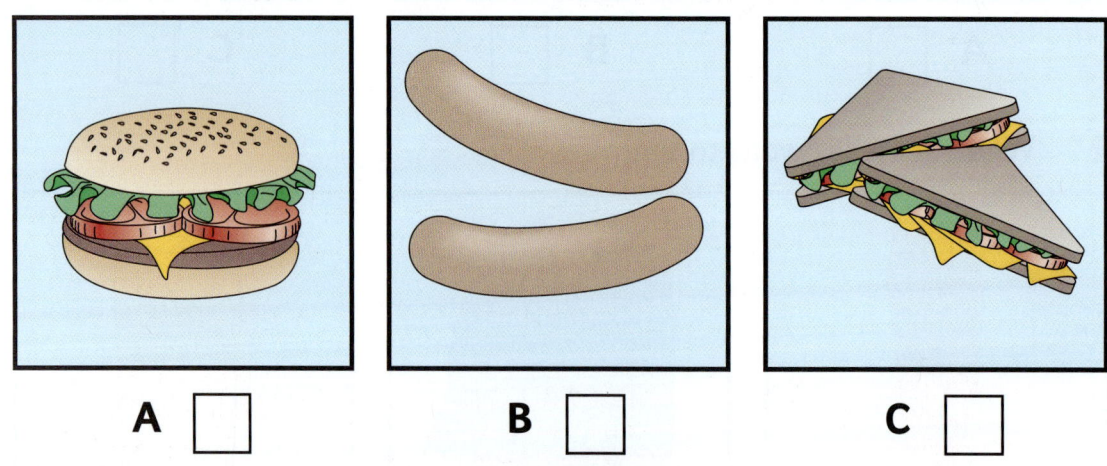

A ☐   B ☐   C ☐

Part 5
– 5 questions –

Listen and colour and draw. There is one example.

Test 2

Reading and Writing

Part 1
– 6 questions –

Look and read. Choose the correct words and write them on the lines. There is one example.

a sandwich

CDs

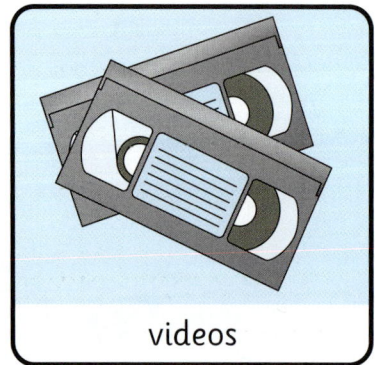

videos

a whale

a dolphin

soup

coffee

a shark

Reading and Writing

Example

This is the biggest animal in the world.   a ....whale.......

Questions

1   You can listen to music with these.   ....

2   We can watch these at home at the
    weekend.   ....

3   On cold days it is good to have
    a hot bowl of this.   ....

4   People are afraid of this animal, which
    lives in the sea.   ....

5   Some people drink this hot, with milk
    and sugar.   ....

6   Put butter and cheese between bread
    and you have one of these.   ....

Part 2
– 6 questions –

Look and read. Write yes or no.

Examples

The man at the table is wearing glasses.   ....yes........

The little girl is carrying a dog.   ....no........

Reading and Writing

Questions

1 The woman between the bookcases is wearing a red dress. ....

2 The cat under the table is looking at the boy. ....

3 One of the boys is playing with a robot. ....

4 The woman at the table is putting on her jacket. ....

5 It's a beautiful sunny day. ....

6 One of the women has got brown curly hair. ....

Part 3
– 6 questions –

Read the text and choose the best answer.

Example

Paul: Hello Sally. How are you?

Sally: (A) I'm very well thanks.
B It's good thanks.
C I'm going to school.

Questions

1 **Paul:** What did you do on your birthday?

   Sally: A It was on Saturday.
   B I had a party at home.
   C Yes, I did.

2 **Paul:** Did you have a cake?

   Sally: A   Yes, I do.
   B   Yes, I have one.
   C   Yes, I did.

3 **Paul:** How many friends came?

   Sally: A   I don't know.
   B   I don't think.
   C   I'm afraid.

4 **Paul:** Have you got any photos of the party?

   Sally: A   Yes, excuse me.
   B   Yes, please.
   C   Yes, they're here.

5 **Paul:** This one's very good.

   Sally: A   Yes, it's well.
   B   Yes, I like it.
   C   Yes, it's ugly.

6 **Paul:** Oh, look, the lesson is starting.

   Sally: A   Oh, I must go.
   B   Good morning.
   C   It's mine.

Part 4
– 7 questions –

Read the story. Choose a word from the box. Write the correct word next to numbers 1–6. There is one example.

Last weekend, I went to the countryside. My father drove the ....car............ on to some grass between two trees. We all got out and **(1)** .... to a field there. I took a picture of some funny black and white **(2)** .... because I love farm animals. Then my father shouted 'Look behind you!' so I did. I **(3)** .... a big horse. It was very near to me. I was afraid and ran to the river and jumped in! My parents laughed. 'The horse doesn't want to hurt you. It's a nice horse,' my mum said. 'Your clothes are **(4)** .... now. Take this towel. And here, give this nice, green **(5)** .... to the horse.' The horse ate it. I was hungry too and I enjoyed our **(6)** .... by the river. We had three different salads, my favourite cheese and some watermelon.

Reading and Writing

Example

car   carried   apple

quiet   wet   picnic

walked   saw   sheep

(7) Now choose the best name for the story.
Tick one box.

Working on the farm   ☐

The new swimming pool   ☐

The horse at the river   ☐

37

Part 5
– 10 questions –

Look at the pictures and read the story. Write words to complete the sentences about the story. You can use 1, 2 or 3 words.

What a nice old woman!

My name's Daisy and I'm ten. Last holiday I wanted to see my grandma. She lives in a small village by the sea. I like it there because I can swim and play on the beach. I went to Grandma's by bus.
First, I went with my mother to the bus stop at the end of our street. I caught the number 3 bus to the big bus station.

Examples

.... Daisy .... is ten.

Daisy's grandmother's house is in ...... a small village ...... that's near the sea.

Questions

1 Daisy likes to .... on the beach.

2 Daisy got on a bus at the end of her ....

3 The number 3 bus went to the ....

Reading and Writing

Then I had to catch another bus – the number 20. But I was hungry. I went to a shop first to buy a chicken sandwich and some lemonade. When I came out, I saw the bus start. I ran and jumped on it. I sat next to an old woman who talked a lot! It was very hot and I went to sleep. When I woke up, I wasn't in my grandmother's village! I was in a big town!

4   Daisy bought a .... to eat because she was hungry.

5   The person next to Daisy on the bus was an ....

6   Daisy slept because it was .... on the bus.

7   When Daisy woke up, the bus was in ....

I was on the wrong bus! I was afraid. The old woman said, 'What's the matter?' I told her my story. We got off the bus and she phoned my grandma. Then she bought me another bus ticket and took me to the right bus – the one that went to my grandma's village.
'Thank you very much!' I said.

8   Daisy was afraid because she was on ....

9   The old woman phoned ....

10 The old woman got a .... for Daisy to go to the right village!

Blank Page

Part 6
– 5 questions –

Read the text. Choose the right words and write them on the lines.

Snakes

Example A lot of people are very afraid ....of........ snakes.

1 They think all snakes .... ugly and want to hurt them. But this is wrong because some snakes are very beautiful

2 and .... don't hurt people. Snakes often

3 .... in the grass or in forests. Some of them

4 eat mice. Some snakes can climb trees very ....

5 and they can swim .... rivers. You must always be careful with snakes and you must never pick them up.

Reading and Writing

Example	to	for	of
1	is	are	were
2	it	she	they
3	live	lives	lived
4	quick	quickly	quicker
5	at	by	in

Test 3
Listening

Part 1
– 5 questions –

Listen and draw lines. There is one example.

Mrs Brown   Peter   Paul   Tom

Mrs Green   Mr Farmer   Sue

Listening

Part 2
– 5 questions –

Listen and write. There is one example.

	Name:	Tom Hill
1	Lives at:	15 .... Street
2	How old:	....
3	Father's name:	....
4	Mother's name:	....
5	What hurts:	....

Test 3

Part 3
– 5 questions –

What did Jim do last week?

Listen and draw a line from the day to the correct picture.

There is one example.

Monday

Tuesday

Wednesday

Thursday

Friday

Saturday

Sunday

Listening

Part 4
– 5 questions –

Listen and tick (✓) the box. There is one example.

Which is Ben's brother's car?

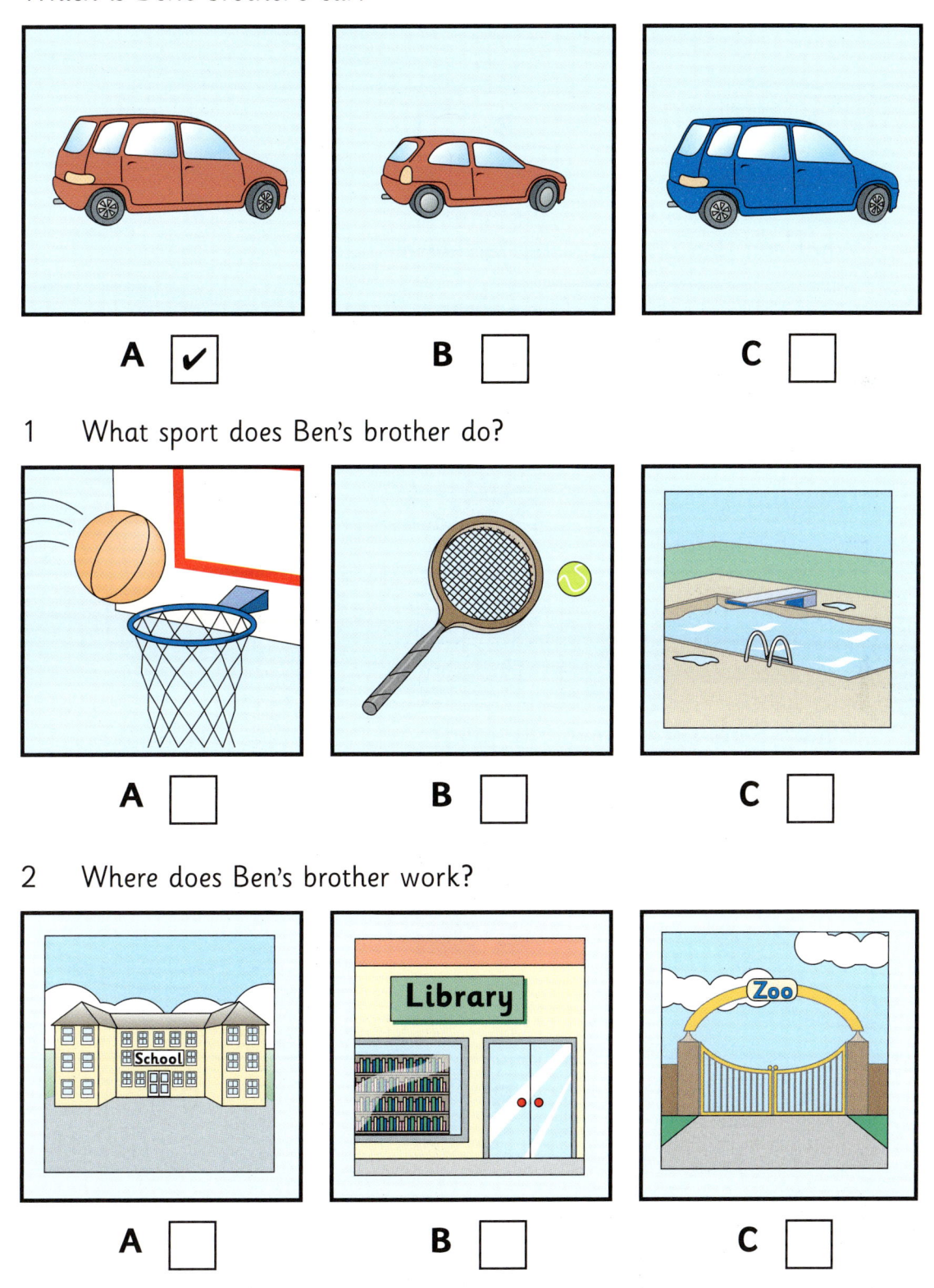

A ✓   B ☐   C ☐

1 What sport does Ben's brother do?

A ☐   B ☐   C ☐

2 Where does Ben's brother work?

A ☐   B ☐   C ☐

3 How did Ben go to his grandparents' house?

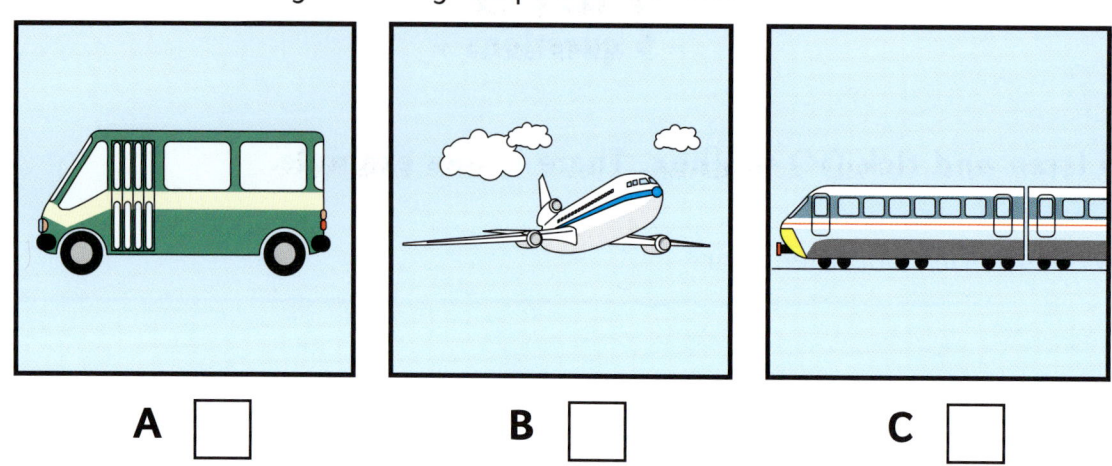

A ☐ B ☐ C ☐

4 What can Ben give his sister for her birthday?

A ☐ B ☐ C ☐

5 What's Ben's sister's favourite food?

A ☐ B ☐ C ☐

Listening

Part 5
— 5 questions —

Listen and colour and draw. There is one example.

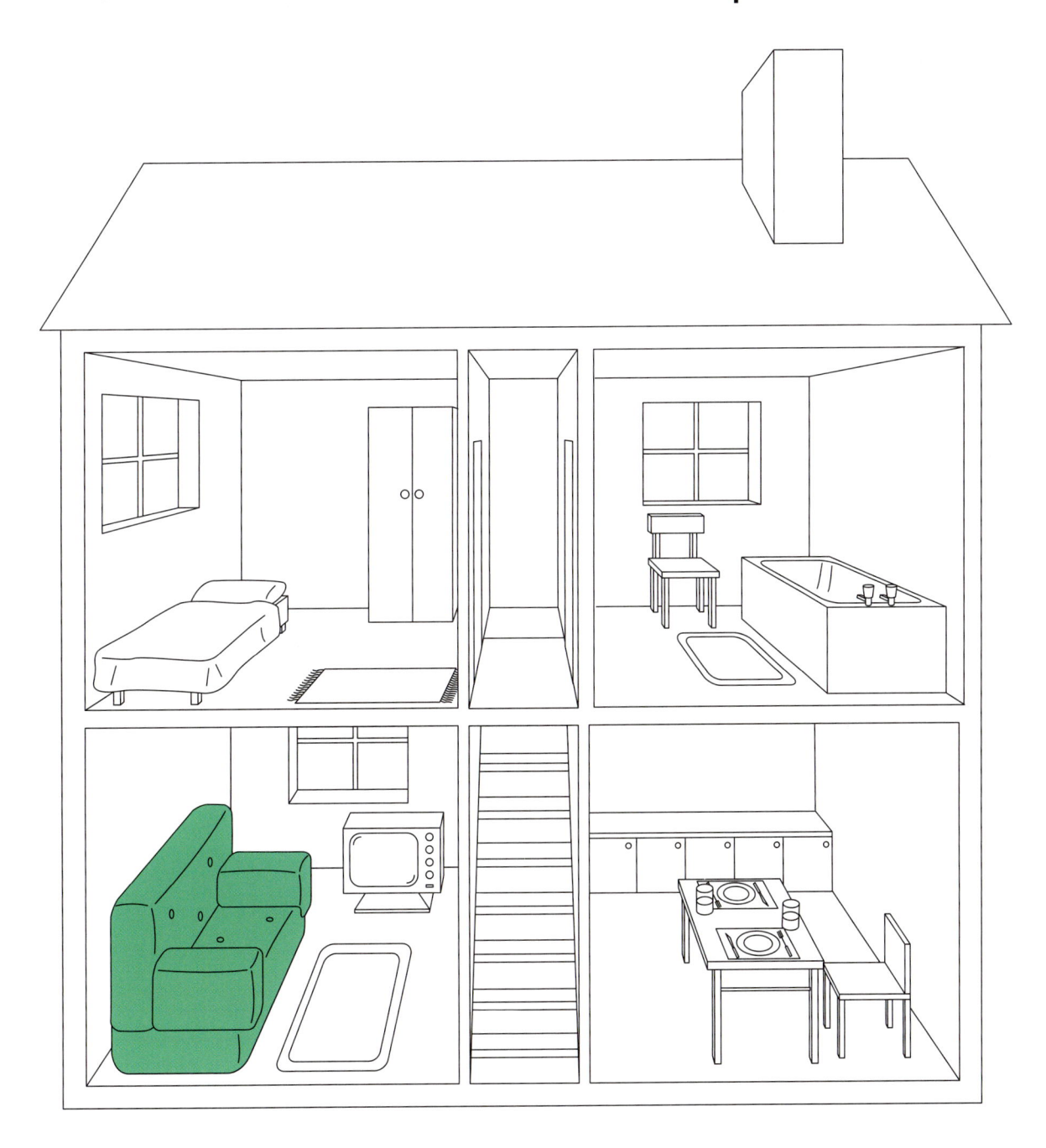

Test 3
Reading and Writing

Part 1
– 6 questions –

Look and read. Choose the correct words and write them on the lines. There is one example.

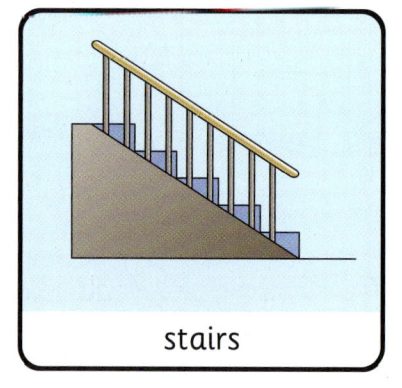

a town

mountains

a cup

stairs

the world

a bottle

a farm

a zoo

Reading and Writing

Example

You can drink tea in this. ....cup.............

Questions

1   More people live here than in a village. ....

2   People like climbing these in the holidays. ....

3   You can buy lemonade in this. ....

4   You find animals like cows and sheep here. ....

5   You need these to go up to the second floor. ....

6   It is big and round and we all live there. ....

Test 3

Part 2
– 6 questions –

Look and read. Write yes or no.

Examples

It's a sunny day. ....yes.................

A white cat is sitting on the wall. ....no.................

Reading and Writing

Questions

1 The teacher is pointing at the dog.   ....

2 A boy with red trousers is riding a bicycle.   ....

3 One of the children has got a pet snake.   ....

4 Three boys are playing with a ball.   ....

5 The girl under the tree is eating.   ....

6 The girl next to the wall is wearing trousers.   ....

Part 3
– 6 questions –

Read the text and choose the best answer.

Example

Bill: Hello Pat. Shall I carry your books?

Pat: A Yes, I shall.
B Yes, they're mine.
(C) Yes, please.

Questions

1 **Bill:** Why didn't you come for table tennis yesterday?

Pat: A And I was ill.
B Because I was tired.
C But I had to go with my mother.

Reading and Writing

2 **Bill:** Do you want to come and see my new kite?

   Pat: A I've got to go home.
                B I want it.
                C I'm not coming.

3 **Bill:** Can you come tomorrow then?

   Pat: A You can come.
                B I'll ask my mum.
                C It's today.

4 **Bill:** Have you got homework to do?

   Pat: A Yes, a lot.
                B Yes, I've got to.
                C I do.

5 **Bill:** Why are you stopping here?

   Pat: A I don't live here.
                B This is my house.
                C I'm not waiting.

6 **Bill:** Here are your books, then.

   Pat: A Oh yes, they are.
                B Oh yes, please.
                C Oh yes, thanks.

Part 4
– 7 questions –

Read the story. Choose a word from the box. Write the correct word next to numbers 1–6. There is one example.

One day last week, Jim got up and went to work. He put on his .... *trousers* .... , shirt and jacket very quietly because his family weren't awake. Then he went to the bathroom, had a shower and cleaned his **(1)** .... He went downstairs to the kitchen and made a cup of **(2)** .... and ate some bread and cheese. Then he picked up his bag and **(3)** .... to work on his bike. He was surprised because the **(4)** .... was very quiet. There were no cars or people there. Jim worked at the library but when he tried to open the **(5)** .... of the library, he couldn't. A man with a dog stopped to talk to him. 'It's Sunday, you know!' he said. 'The library isn't open today!' Jim **(6)** .... 'Oh great!' he said, 'I can go back to bed!'

Example

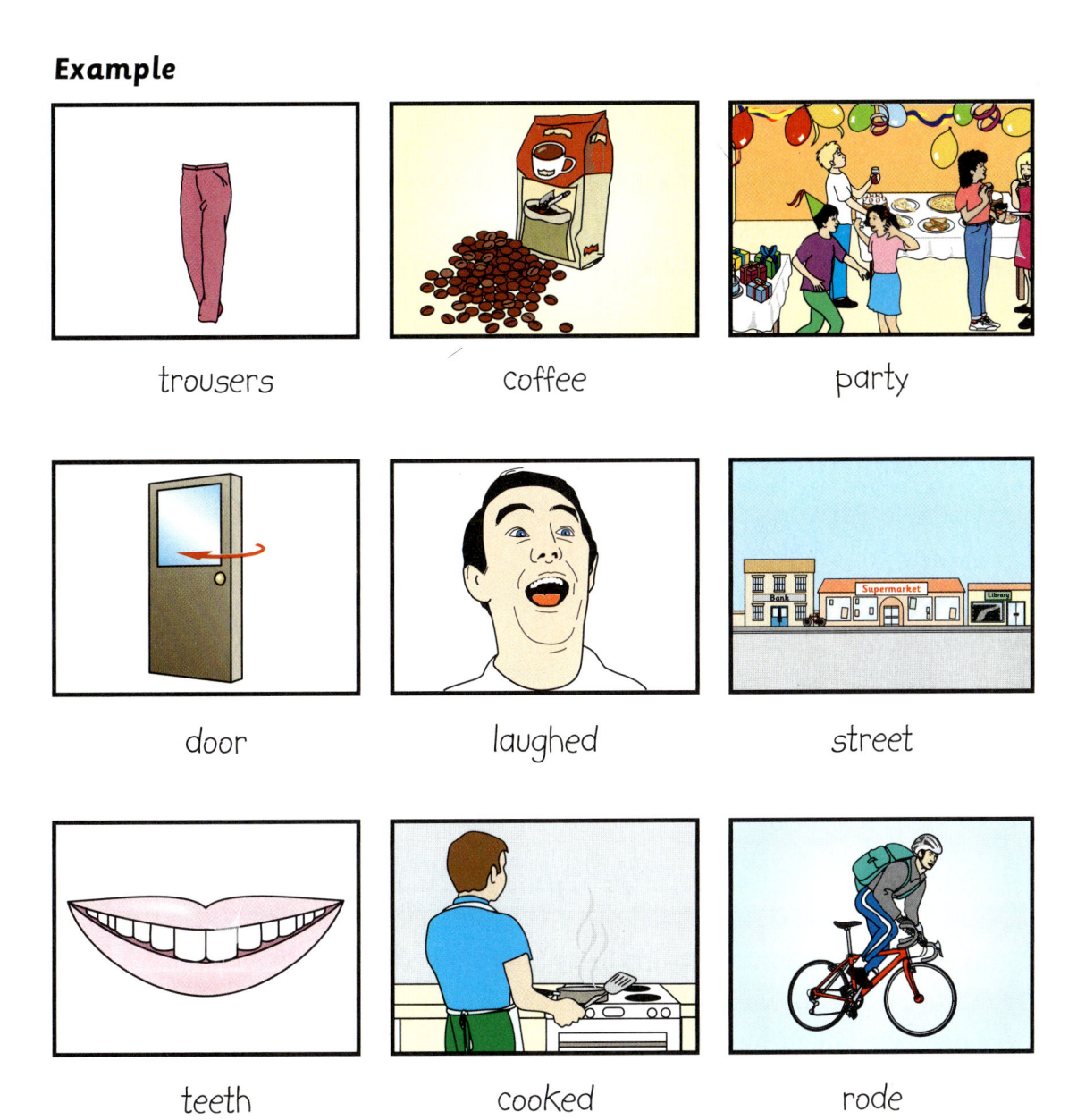

trousers

coffee

party

door

laughed

street

teeth

cooked

rode

(7) Now choose the best name for the story.
Tick one box.

Jim makes a mistake ☐

Jim's big breakfast ☐

Jim's new friend ☐

Test 3

Part 5
– 10 questions –

Look at the pictures and read the story. Write words to complete the sentences about the story. You can use 1, 2 or 3 words.

Pasta the Parrot

Mary's uncle and aunt came to her house last week. They gave her a beautiful parrot. It was blue and yellow. Mary was very happy with her new pet. She called him 'Pasta'. Mary's aunt told her, 'Parrots eat fruit.' Mary's uncle said, 'Parrots can talk. You have to teach Pasta some words, Mary'.

Examples

.......*Last week*....... Mary's uncle and aunt went to see her.

The present that they brought Mary was ......*a beautiful parrot*...... .

Questions

1 The colours of the parrot were ....

2 .... was the name that Mary gave the parrot.

3 Mary can teach her new pet some ....

Reading and Writing

First, Mary taught the parrot to say 'Pasta' and 'Hello'. Then he learned to say 'Mary', 'Yes', 'No' and 'Lunch'! Then Pasta learned more words. On Saturday, Mary's mother opened the living room door and asked Mary and her younger brother, Fred, 'What do you want to eat for lunch?' Fred shouted, 'Pasta!' The parrot was there with them and he thought, 'Oh no! Fred wants to eat me,' and he flew outside.

4   The first two words that Pasta learned were ....

5   Fred, who was Mary's .... , wanted to eat pasta for lunch.

6   Pasta was afraid and .... out the window.

Mary and Fred ran out to the garden, but they couldn't see Pasta. Then their mother shouted, 'Oh! He's here in the kitchen.'
The children went to see. Pasta had a grape in his mouth and then he gave it to Mary's mother. She laughed and said, 'I know you want to tell us something. Is it, please eat fruit and not Pasta?' The parrot jumped up and down, 'Yes, yes,' he said!

7   The children couldn't find the parrot in ....

8   Their mother found Pasta in ....

9   Pasta gave .... to Mary and Fred's mum.

10 When Pasta said .... , he jumped up and down.

Blank Page

Part 6
– 5 questions –

Read the text. Choose the right words and write them on the lines.

Zoos

Example | Some big towns have zoos. .... *Inside* .... a zoo you can find a lot of animals. There is often a hot house for snakes,

1 | .... house for birds and a big lake for ducks and

2 | fish. Some zoos .... got a big field with

3 | elephants, lions or tigers. .... is often a

4 | shop or a playground too. Children like .... to the zoo in their holidays because they can see the animals, ride on the

5 | elephants or give food .... the monkeys.

Reading and Writing

Example	Inside	Outside	About
1	some	another	any
2	do	are	have
3	They	There	It
4	went	going	go
5	at	for	to

Blank Page

Test 1

Speaking

Find the difference

Test 1 Speaking

Story

Test 1 Speaking

Find the different ones

Blank Page

Test 2

Speaking

Find the difference

69

Test 2 Speaking

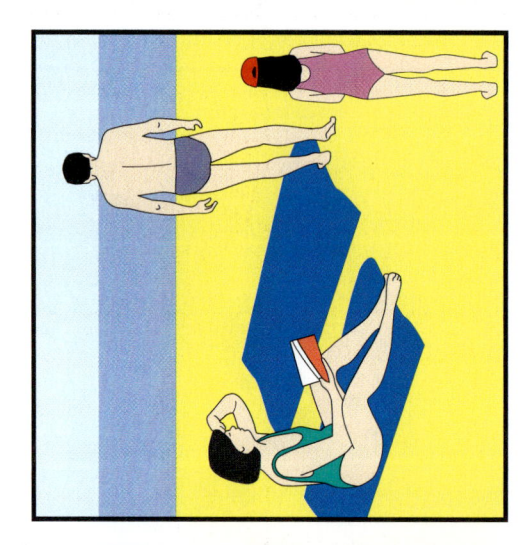

Story

Find the different ones

Blank Page

Test 3

Speaking

Find the difference

Test 3 Speaking

Story

Test 3 Speaking

Find the different ones